First American Edition 1994 by
Kane/Miller Book Publishers
La Jolla, California

Originally published in Japan under the title
Hana no ana no hanashi by
Fukuinkan Shoten, Publishers, Inc., Tokyo, 1981
Copyright ©1981 Genichiro Yagyu
American text copyright ©Kane/Miller Book Publishers

All rights reserved. For information contact:
Kane/Miller Book Publishers
P.O. Box 8515, La Jolla, CA 92038-8515
www.kanemiller.com

First American Paperback Edition, 2005
Library of Congress Catalog Card Number 93-80448
ISBN 1-929132-82-4

Printed and bound in Singapore by Tien Wah Press Pte., Ltd.
1 2 3 4 5 6 7 8 9 10

The Holes In Your Nose

By Genichiro Yagyu

Translated by Amanda Mayer Stinchecum

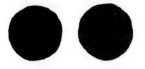

A CURIOUS NELL BOOK

Kane/Miller
BOOK PUBLISHERS

The holes in my nose are bigger than hers.

But they're not nearly as big as Grandpa's.

When I'm old, will the holes in my nose be like that?

I can't wait to find out.

Holes in the nose come in all different sizes and shapes.

Now, everybody, look up and show the person reading this book the holes in your nose.

You with the moustache—no need to open your mouth.

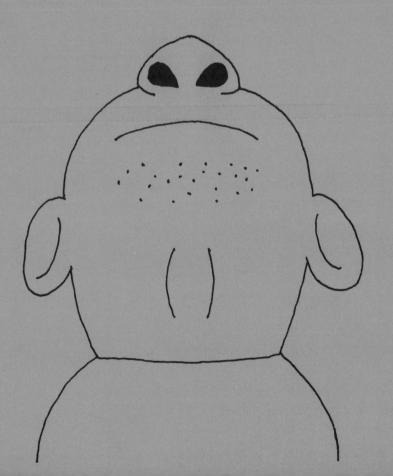

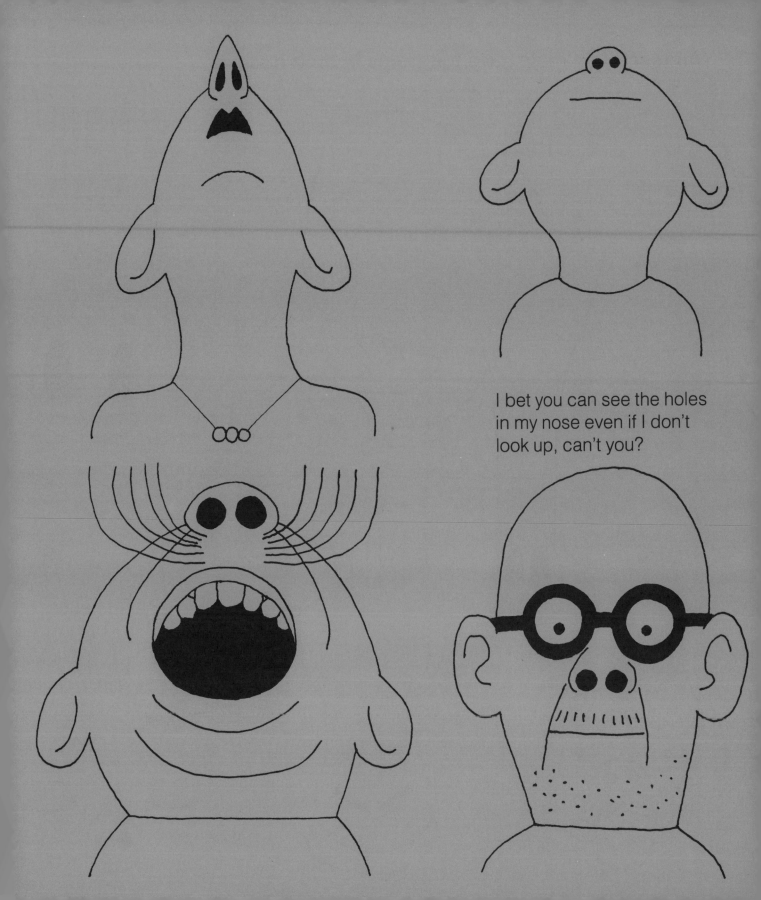

I bet you can see the holes in my nose even if I don't look up, can't you?

Almost all animals have two holes in their noses.

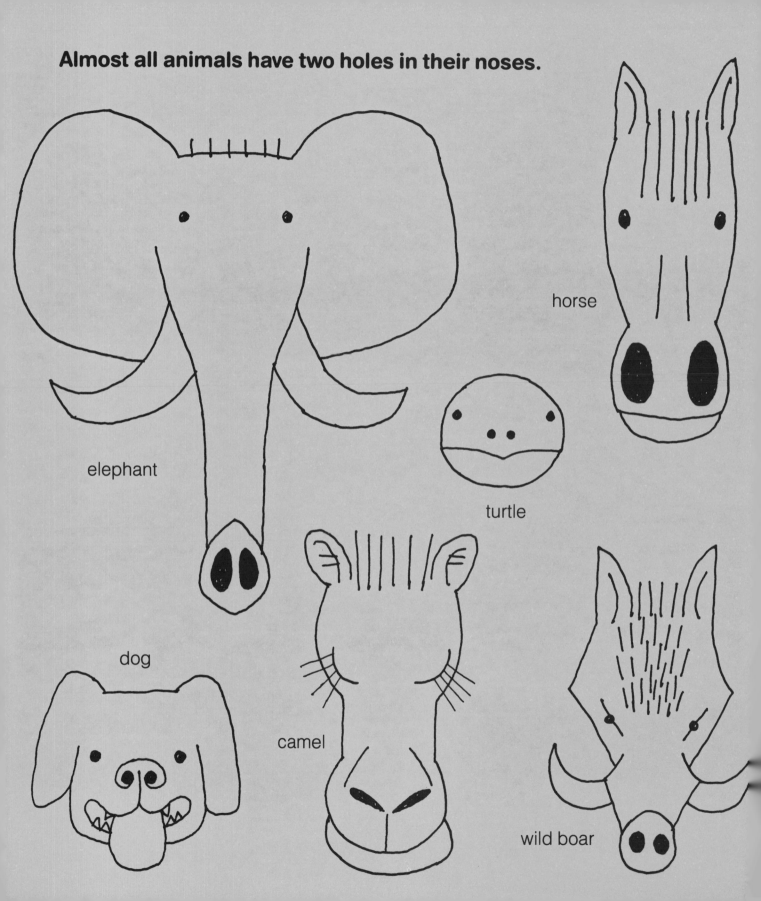

elephant

horse

turtle

dog

camel

wild boar

But some have only one.

It's right here.

The one hole in a dolphin's nose is on top of its head.

A seal can open up the holes in its nose wide, or squeeze them closed. So when it dives under, water doesn't get in its nose.

The hippopotamus, too, can pop open the holes in its nose really wide or snap them shut. Very useful, those holes in its nose.

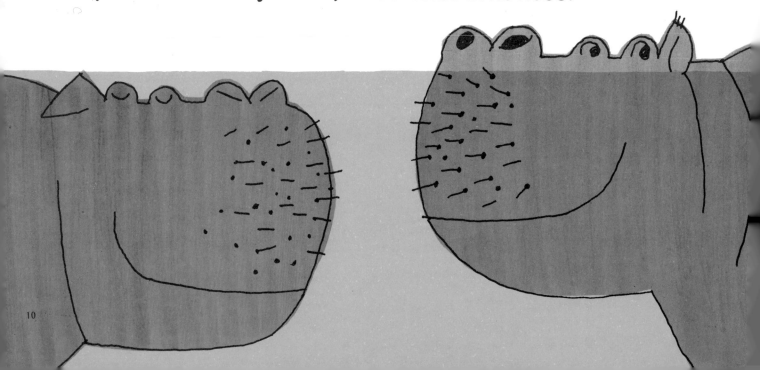

We can make the holes in our noses
bigger and smaller, too.
But only a little.

We breathe through the holes in our noses, sucking in the air, then pushing it out. This is the most important thing the holes in our noses do.

**Of course when we open our mouths,
we can breathe through our mouths or our noses.**

What about the hole in
the lid of the tea kettle?
Is it a nose hole too?

"Ugh!"
"Poo!"

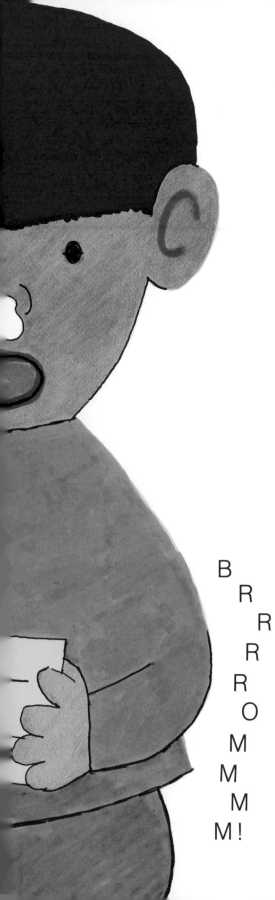

When the holes in your nose get stuffed up, you can't smell anything.

"Wed the holes in my dose are sdubbed ub,
I candt sbell id eved wed I fart."

"PU. What a stink!"

B
R
R
R
R
O
M
M
M
M!

**When the holes in your nose get stuffed up,
the words you say become harder to understand.**

"By dose is all stubbed ub. Id'z dime for be to go to bed dow.
Good dight."

When the holes in your nose get stuffed up,
it's harder to say m's and n's.

Hold your nose and try saying,
"Na ne nu nay no, ma me moo may mo."

Hairs grow in the holes in your nose.

Nose hairs catch tiny bits of dirt from the air you breathe in.

You don't have to let your nose hairs grow as long as this man's. Not that there's anything wrong with it . . .

A ACHOOO!

When large bits of dirt get in your nose, you blow them out by sneezing.

Boogers collect in the holes in our noses.
Boogers are a mixture of dirt and mucus.
They're like little balls.

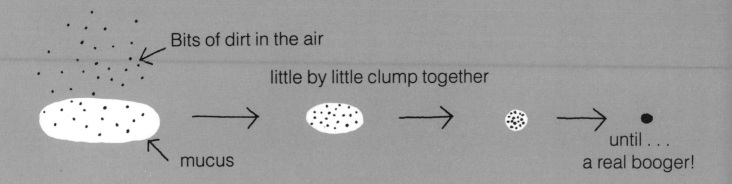

Bits of dirt in the air

little by little clump together

mucus

until . . .
a real booger!

Boogers are made from dirt, so they're dirty.
Even if you line them up neatly like this, they're still dirty.

There is always moisture in your nose, so it's damp inside.
When you catch a cold, there's more moisture than usual.
It becomes mucus and drips out.

"Say, gorilla!
Did you know your
nose is running?
Do you want
a tissue?"

"I don't need one."

"What are you
going to do?"

"Let it dry
then pick it off
and eat it."

"Ugh! Yuck!"

If you pick your nose too roughly, you can get a nosebleed.

"Look! It's bleeding!"

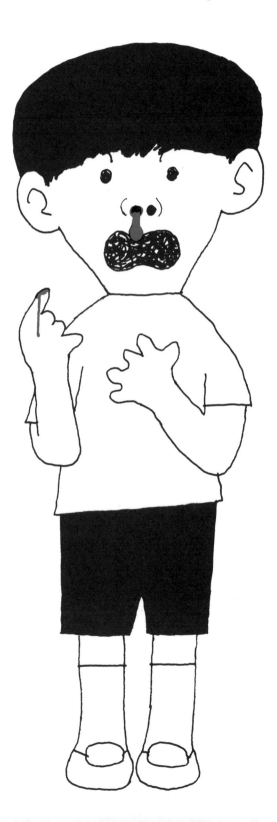

Nosebleeds can happen for many reasons.

Like when you get hit in the nose.

Or even when you're not doing anything, sometimes it will bleed.

Usually a nosebleed will stop if you hold your nose and sit still for ten minutes or so. If it doesn't, you should have a doctor look at it.

What is the inside of your nose like?

There are two holes in your nose,
so the inside of your nose is
divided in two all the way back.

The inside of your nose and the
inside of your mouth are connected
at the back of your throat.

right nose hole

The inside of your nose is full of funny shaped bumps.
The air you breathe in passes between these bumps.

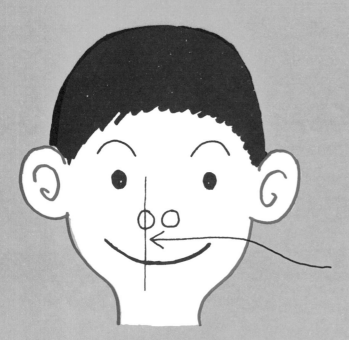

nose hairs

mouth

The big picture on the right
is a side view of this part
of the inside of your nose.

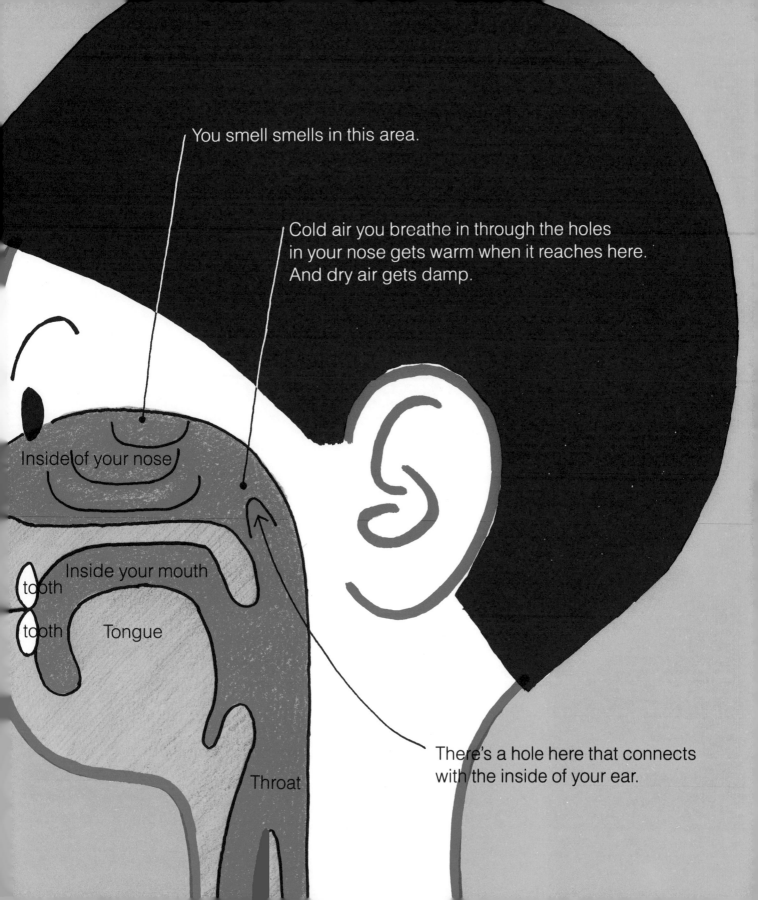

**The holes in your nose are not pockets.
So don't put pebbles, peas, erasers,
pencils or anything else in the holes in your nose.**

"Don't do it."

"They say
you're not
supposed
to do it . . ."

If you fill up the holes in your nose with morning glory seeds, the
seeds will swell up and begin to sprout. Your nose will hurt a lot.
And that would be terrible!

There are lots of other holes
in your body besides the
holes in your nose.

The holes in your ears.
your mouth,
the hole in your behind,
the hole where pee
comes out.

All the holes in your body
are very important.
You should always keep
them clean.

When the holes in your nose look like this, it means, THE END!

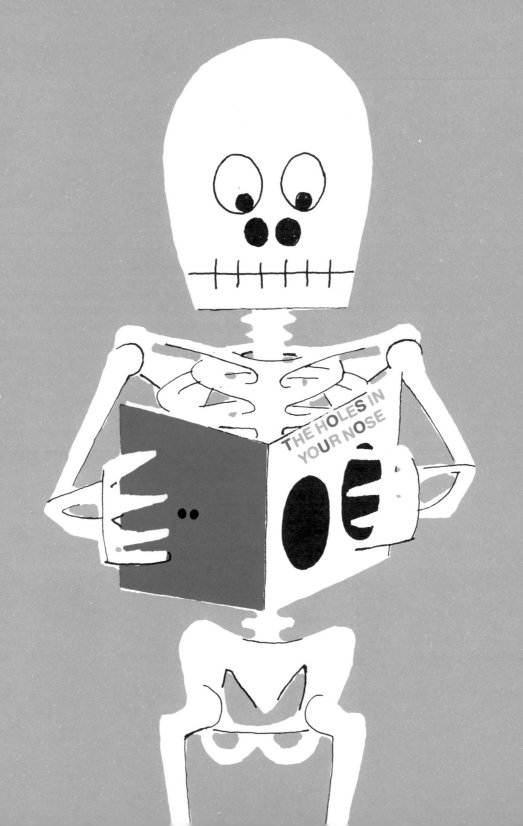